love and other company

celia sinclair
e.m. handly

Two Ten Press

love and other company copyright © 2022 Celia Sinclair. All rights reserved. No part of this book may be used or reproduced in any manner whatsoever without written permission from the publisher except for the use of brief quotations in reviews.

E.M Handly
writing as
Celia Sinclair

Two Ten Press
twotenpress@gmail.com

Print ISBN: 978-1-7367415-7-3
Print ISBN: 978-1-7367415-8-0

www.emhandly.com
www.celiasinclair.net

To all the men I loved, even if only briefly.

contents

eric
down under
brian
growth
jason
mike

I open my hands
and offer you
my heart

eric

like a composer
creating a masterpiece
your hands gently play
across my skin

each finger
a note of awareness
every touch
another cord

your lips playfully
sing their song to mine

each kiss
a harmonious lyric
every breath
a part of the tune

bodies rhythmically
swaying to the beat

am I a fool
to want to hear it
play again

- making music

celia sinclair & e.m. handly

—♡—

you speak of the future
one we could possibly share
my imagination runs wild
with your comments

I can see our home
puppy roaming aimlessly
in the yard while I tend
to the flowers

the scent of dinner
wafting through the air
awaiting your arrival

falling asleep in your arms
waking to your smile
the next morning

random picture shows
of a life together
continuously
replay in my mind

oh how you make me
want to love you

- here after

love and other company

intoxicating he is
undeniably intoxicating

I long for the desire
the honesty his eyes reflect

those electric blue eyes
how they support
every word he speaks

the pessimist I am
I try to remain coherent

should I succumb
to this drunkenness
I may never be sober again

- stupor

blue skies
warm sand
you and I
hand in hand

no worries
no stress
never an issue
to be pressed

always free
forever open
actually doing
instead of hoping

- ideal

love and other company

they lay in the sand
in complete sexual bliss

the water caressing them
before returning to the ocean

each reaching exotic fulfillment
he ever so gently declares
I love you

and then she awakens

- only a dream

celia sinclair & e.m. handly

I am not with you
yet your scent
burns my nose

not with you
still taste the salt
from your skin

I am not with you
yet I can feel the touch
of your hands on mine

not with you
but hear your voice
flow from your lips

your presence continuously
replays in my mind
oh how I wish you were aware

- if you only knew

love and other company

what a beautiful man
you portrayed yourself to be

so kind and gentle
so loving and caring
so inclined to give me
everything

it's hard to fathom
you played with my emotions
and I was so naïve to let you

how could you receive
such satisfaction
from breaking my heart
with your deceit

- two-faced

you're here but you're not
if you only knew what it took
to keep me

you continue to falter
but I never infer
suppose it's my fault
chastise me for opening
my heart

how can you not
take advantage
how in the hell
can you not
understand

- blind

so vividly I see you
standing there with your
cool, sexy demeanor
somewhat arrogant
dressed head to toe in Tommy

your icy blue eyes
screaming in agony
how bad you wanted me
I enter your embrace
longing to feel the love
I felt for you

but I always knew
I could never
have your heart

- memory

I fear I will do it again.

I try to remind myself
it's too complicated
too demanding
it hurts too much!

What if once again I fall
and continue falling
all the while enjoying
this intense feeling
that has taken over me?

What if –

the repercussions of the past
aren't enough to keep me
from venturing that far?

Even more terrifying –

what if I am led there
only to take the journey alone?

- afraid of love

down under

as smoothly as the ink
flows from my pen
I've longed for the words
to form from my lips
everything my mind wants to say
and my heart aches to tell you

as long as the ocean
has kissed the sand
I've wanted to taste
the salt from your lips
in an eternal kiss of passion

long as the moon caresses our dreams
my desire to know your every thought
every fear – every facet of your being
grows with each breath I take

as sure as the sun will rise tomorrow
we will share our bodies and our souls
the very day me meet

- love from afar

you feel the suns warmth
wishing to worship him for life
the slightest glance of the moon
you fall under his enchantment

one moment you're feeling
instincts of love in your heart
first glimpse of paranoia
you totally disregard all
positive feelings
of intimacy

at times have such confidence
nothing can penetrate you
but can be so naïve
only to have your heart
crushed

how long will this scared little girl
continue to hide
from who she really is
and what she really wants

- uncertainty

love and other company

what is it that makes me
want you so bad
dares my heart to skip a beat
forces the deep recesses of my mind
to dream of you

is it because you're
such a challenge

maybe –
just maybe it's because I know
there are no strings attached

when I'm with you it feels…

or could this all be
a mere release

- danny

It's almost time to close now.
You come in, sit at the bar
and ask me what I'm doing after work.

You've already had a few drinks,
enough to relax you anyway.

Maybe I intimidate you?
Has it been a month already?
No phone calls or invites in between.
Of course, that's typical for you.

You wait patiently until I'm done
in hopes that I'll follow you home
so we can perform that meaningless
deed we've always done.

What if for once
I resisted your advances?
Would you continue
to pursue?

And if you didn't
would I really care?

- 2:30 am

is it possible to love
more than one person

not necessarily lovers
but that *one*
who makes you feel alive
free
happy

we're raised to believe
you get one chance
yet question the survival rate

hence the confusion
mistrust
jealousy
comparisons
and broken hearts

could a love truly be so strong
no other could ever
compare

- monogamy

I nearly forgot
what I truly wanted

after all I've done
you still love me

                                - *ryan*

love and other company

because you are beautiful
I love you now and always

you don't deserve what I did
and I'm trying to find a way
to forgive myself

because you are beautiful
you'll always be in my heart

because it's the right
thing to do
I have to let you go

- undeserved

I know you would
be good for me
so why
do I push you away?

I made a fool of myself.
Danny is a lost soul.
I know that now.

I admit I'm lonely
but I can't be with you
out of mere
convenience.

- timing

love and other company

he came to me
from the moonlit sky
carried me into the air
away from danger

we escaped to his land
and his kind
those of eternal youth
beauty and strength

it was then that I knew
I belonged with him

this was my fate
my destiny
my home

how I longed
for his sweet mouth
to strike my neck
share the power he held

but he left me
to be mortal once again

now I await his return
for him to see
this was meant to be

- night angel

you've been there
for longer than
I could conceive

how long have we
seen each other
and looked beyond

- donnie

it was nice to hear from you

even if it was only because
you wanted me to write
your smut
the kind that would
line your pockets nicely

I'm flattered actually
but wasn't it you
who told me some time ago

– you already
had the privilege
of spreading my legs –

as we sat on your sofa
drinking cocktails you said
you're not really the type of girl
I'd take home to mom

and you smiled at me
as if I should understand

- kenny

how does it feel
when you meet someone
who doesn't shun your rarity

be able to look in the mirror
admiring every exquisite part
of everything
that is you

how does it feel
to walk in a room
full of hungry eyes
and deadly lips
hoping their whispers
are directed elsewhere

and even if they aren't
how does it feel
not to care

- insecure

love and other company

you're no different
you want what they all want
and never give in return

spread my legs
but never willing
to expand my mind

I am not tied to you

you're no more interested
than the others
until you see me
with someone else

I'm not a whore

you're just upset
I'm worthy
of someone else's time

I'm not a bitch

you're just confused
as to how I can survive
without you

- bret

I fell in love today
we've met
yet we have not

but I've felt your
gentleness in the breeze
whispering upon my face

seen your strength
in an army of ants marching
carrying ten times their weight

experienced your scent
with the rise of spring flowers
felt your warmth
in the noon day sun

heard your voice
your thoughts
with each new encounter
another conversation

in my heart I know
that with each new day
I continue to create you

- soul mate

faces spinning through the air
thoughts flailing

constant overwhelming ideas
wanting to explore
every mind

if only I could enter
for a moment
and explore the core

- longing

celia sinclair & e.m. handly

---

a roaring ocean of bitter waves
her heart is
forever angry and cold

the whitecaps of her tears
whirlwinds of despair
have long awaited
a ship to hoist his anchor

only then will she be calm
no longer a mad sea

- restless

I feel as if I want to
get closer to you
I'm afraid and undecided
what to do.

I fear if I tell you what
I am thinking
you'll turn and walk
without even blinking.

The way you look at me
the way you touch
I think about it
all too much.

I wish I could tell you
all that's in my head
yet here I sit
driving myself insane
instead.

- silent uncertainty

maybe having
your heart broken
and being alone
isn't so bad

the experience of
giving your soul and
being betrayed in return
can be quite a blessing

after all
it has provoked my mind
to create these great
many thoughts
that transform into the ink
from this pen

hasn't it

- effect

love and other company

what would it be like
to find my one true love

the pure ecstasy two people feel
when they do nothing more
than look in each other's eyes

- knowing

celia sinclair & e.m. handly

I just want to be
that caring, unique
and free-spirited soul

desperately fighting to emerge
from antiquated ideals
surrounding happiness

they taunt and criticize
as if they are perfect

I imagine it's a reflection
of their own morbidly miserable lives

in the event of self-gratification
I am branded immoral
impure
slut!

this is my novel
don't read it
if you disagree

- controversial

you see yourself
hear yourself speak
take actions based on emotions
you've told yourself
are okay to feel

ones that come natural
ones already made
and not yet remembered
ones recalled
through the eyes of another

believing if they had a glimpse
they would laugh out loud
but hope they deeply ponder

- understanding

I will be strong
I refuse to reveal
my inner most self
to anyone

I don't believe
there are many people
I can trust
wholeheartedly

- strength

the lords and
the new creatures
would have smiled
on this first kiss

springing the imagination
of bodies tangled
fantastically exploring
body and spirit

- brian

brian

I can't concentrate
for you consume my thoughts

I try to divert my mind
yet I am led to you
once again

disturbingly invigorating
undeniably soothing

every part of my being
from the depths of my soul
to every breath that parts these lips

you are the core
of my very existence

- consumed

celia sinclair & e.m. handly

---♡---

skin on skin
lips locked

tongues flailing
breathing ecstasy

taste the sweet nectar
breath the flavorful aroma

bask in the winds of emotion

- rapture

love and other company

have you walked a day
inside my heart
visited me in my dreams

have you felt the vibrations
of my thoughts
the energy of my soul
swimming in the earth's aura

you must have heard
the waves of electricity
whispering to you
leading you
to my embrace

- prophetic

celia sinclair & e.m. handly

I will be your strength
whenever you feel weak.
I will show you positive
for every negative peak.

I will be the smile
for every tear you cry.
I will have the answer
for every question why.

I will pick you up
if ever you should fall.
I'll be the one to answer
whatever time you call.

I will be your comfort
whenever you feel pain.
I will be the sun
to save you from the rain.

I will be your truth
for every lie that's told.
I will be your everything
from now until we're old.

- promise

do you believe
in soul mates

believe in a love
that challenges
eternity

a love so exquisite
hearts and souls
joined together
as if
they never parted

magnificently
creating itself
anew

travelers
on a mystifying journey
to exotic places
never ventured

only to remember
somehow
they had been there
before

- complete

you've entered my coven
the secret world of the nymph

heard my chants
felt my magic
watched the shadows
play a ritual dance
invoking this blessed sanction

existing beyond space
time
matter

I have cast my spell upon you love
one that is bound
never to be broken

- bewitched

love and other company

for years I followed the rainbow
in search of my pot of gold

walked the yellow brick road
in ruby red slippers
trying to find my way home

in every journey I saw rejection
what I thought was love
became depression

a romance would come
next day would leave
somehow I kept my faith
in love I still believed

you've opened my mind
wiped the tears from my eyes
reminded my heart
true love never lies

- oz

celia sinclair & e.m. handly

days I can't be near you
are entirely too long

nights you're not next to me
uncomfortably cold
and tomorrow
can't come soon enough

silent tears before I sleep
begging for the day
I no longer feel this pain

love and other company

now that you're here
I can't imagine otherwise

I never want to see
the day you disappear

as if you're a pleasant dream
I fear I'll wake from

the missing link of my soul
returned to me
never to be taken away

- please stay

for one to be in love
with your thoughts

want to enter
the deepest realm
of your mind

intrigued by the very depth
of your soul

a fantastical experience
magical
poetical

- connection

listen to the ocean whisper
sweet nothings to the sand
shhh...
can you hear it

the sound of his waves
envelope her milky white body
for all time to come

hear them sing to each other
the song of ever after

dance my prince
your future has been told

- something like forever

we've lived a life
together before

it's a beautiful thing
to have found each other
again

- fate

love and other company

I wish I could
climb inside you

the closer we become
the closer I want us to be

like trying to capture the moon
in all its essence
chasing the sun in lavish circles
forever basking in the light
of eternal love

- in your head

someone has filled
your precious heart with pain
made you believe many untruths

a frozen pool of black
has unleashed its evil
crushing all the beauty
that thrives in your being

squeezing the life breath
from the very thing I cherish
rest assured love
you'll hurt no longer

- separation

love and other company

and god lay this
precious gift upon her
to love for all eternity

with that first breath
she shed a tear
in the presence of
what she thought
to be a mere façade

the never-ending desire
she had created
for herself

- fantasy

I'm not going to tell you
I love you more than her.

I'm not going to demand
you make a choice.

I'm not going to
make you feel bad
for not knowing
what to do.

No matter how much
I hurt right now,
I refuse to make you
hurt more.

Whether or not
you break my heart,
the weight of that decision
is yours alone to carry.

- goodbye

when I see you
I'm a girl again

there is still a curiosity
something mysteriously
challenging

I realize I can
never have you
as a whole

we all want what
we can't have

the more unattainable
the faster we chase it

but I wanted you
even when I knew
you were mine

- waiting

the moment I felt
I was over you
you managed to walk
back into my life

no particular purpose
no devious intentions
just present
once again

I try to justify it
try and figure out
why you're here

in reality
there's no explanation
our souls simply
connect

- unintentional

love and other company

could you ever accept my love
or has your heart been hurt too badly

I tried to show it to you
at one time thought I succeeded

it took a long time
for someone to make you believe
it doesn't exist

if you let me
I can help you remember
what it feels like

- patient

celia sinclair & e.m. handly

you left unexpectedly
intentionally

all I think about
is you

can you tell me
what it feels like
to be the core
of my very existence

every feeling
that has touched
this skin

the definition of
every word that
has left these lips

the very beat
of the drum
inside this heart

- everything

My heart tells me
you still love me.

You're terrified.

I don't blame you.

I don't know why I try.

I continue to wait patiently.

Why are you here?

I remember how it sounded
when you said you loved me.

You're hurt and confused
but please if there isn't
a snowball's chance in hell
just say so.

- hanging on

Why do I wish to dwell on the things that are totally out of my control, such as how another person feels about me? I could love someone with all my heart and never know whether or not they give a damn about me. Yet, I continue to concern myself with this complexity. If I love and I am not loved back, that is their loss. Forgive me if I see too much good in people. I refuse to see differently. I believe everyone can love.

Everyone harbors that need to need someone else. Why does no one need or love me? Why do *you* not need me – love me? Everyone has that one chance in their life and I feel that chance is here and now, with you. It's just a matter of convincing you.

How can you not know
how you feel?

Even more peculiar –
how can I still feel at all?

The anger has disappeared
but the hurt continues to linger.

Is there a reason
I saw you tonight?

Or is it just a reminder
we were never meant to be?

- fluke

what does your mind
say to you

what questions
do you ask yourself

what thoughts does
your heart convey

if it can at all

or is the damage so extreme
it is irreparable

- broken

growth

I miss the stroke of your hand
against my cheek

your smile
your face
the way your eyes cry
passion

missed the nights
of drifting to sleep in your arms
waking faintly to your kiss

bodies breathing
laughing
exploring
rhythmically reaching
oneness

missed those words
that ever-so-gently follow

- missing you

celia sinclair & e.m. handly

I loved you once
enough to give up my soul.
At one time felt complete
bits and pieces became a whole.

A bond had formed
one I thought was never-ending.
Reality -
slap to my face -
simply lust, love still pending.

I was there for you
given everything I had
still here I sit alone
with my pen and my pad.

I loved you once
I know I will love again.
No longer be alone
with my pad and my pen.

- healing

You matter.
Your thoughts matter.
No pressure.
No pressure.
You are beautiful.

---

the moon lights the sky
seagulls sing their song

the clouds paint pictures
that dance in the reflection of the lake

all is at peace
with the world

- john doe

are you interested

can you feel my intrigue
hear the palpitations
of my heart

I dare not
appear desperate

I wait patiently
for a sign

- unfamiliar

love and other company

don't think I'll ever know
how it feels to be loved
not sure I'm supposed to

the meaning of life varies
from soul to soul
some are here to remind us
of who we don't want to be

others to intrigue
inspire
remind us to never stop
wondering
wanting
all that is good in the world

sadly more than necessary
inflict heartache
pain
suffering

maybe that's why I'm here

to show as many as I can
how it feels to be loved and adored
and to fill as many hearts as I can
with some sort of happiness

the day I accept this beautiful gift
is the day I am free

- growth

love and other company

unconsciously aware
I see your beautiful face
smell your sweet fragrance
feel your velvet touch

taste the salt from your lips
I even hear you speak
my name

all senses awake
I breath you in

I dare not exhale

for fear of losing you
again

- wishful presence

the fear of growing old and alone
tears at my heart
as I cry the last tear from losing you

the thought of never knowing
what it feels like
to be one's very reason for living
terrifies me

a mere fantasy
consuming my subconscious
periodically revealing itself
to the conscious

simply to remind myself
I still believe it exists

- loneliness

love and other company

---♡---

Until I find you, my soul shall not rest.
My dreams forever be haunted.

---♡---

someone has bestowed a curse
upon me

taken my future and kept it
for themselves

a future I never
thought I wanted

my heart weeps
knowing what I desire
can be mine
only in my sleep

- afflicted

would it matter
if I were or were not here

where would these
so-called friends
get their whiskey

where would they get their beer

there is nothing more pathetic
than listening to drunken rhetoric

it's never mattered who's here

as long as there's whiskey
and as long as there's beer

- don

it doesn't matter what I do
there's selfish people
just like you

we sit here all night
I've told you things that might
we both have other obligations
should certain things interfere
we raise complications

if we please ourselves
there can be no reservations
only explicit conversations

- tempting

why does everyone
think I'm so different

maybe I am

I'm not afraid to express
the deep emotions
raging from the abyss
inside of me

screaming to be free

- my reality

please refrain from telling me
I'm beautiful
I may want you to tell me again

please refrain from saying
you enjoy my company
I may continue to accompany you

please refrain from telling me
I'm special
I may begin to feel as if I am

please refrain from telling me
you're falling for me
I may end up falling harder

please refrain
from making love to me
because it may turn into
just that

- restraint

love and other company

I remain surrounded
in a pit of resentment
I can no longer blame
anyone else

beneath these walls
of fiery contempt
I search for a path
to release myself

round and round
in circles I go
my head is spinning
and ready to blow

I cry for help
yet no one can hear
then a voice whispers
it's up to you my dear

still I wander – searching
thinking – dreaming – hoping
to relieve the fear and the doubt
without aimlessly moping

is there no way out
of this miserable trap
find the man of my dreams
move away perhaps

one day I shall rise
leave this all behind
love and security
I do intend to find

- free

is love worth sacrificing
your needs and wants
to fulfill those of the one
you crave

does the cost of the heartache
the confusion
questions of loyalty
and faithfulness
outweigh
loneliness

is it worth your heart
being crushed
left to heal and scar
only to do it again
and again

- chance

celia sinclair & e.m. handly

---

there is a price
on everyone's heart

and it gets pretty expensive

- bounty

love and other company

I found my soul mate once
made him the core of everything
that I was
everything I was
to become

how can I allow myself
to feel so much
knowing in the end
he'll hurt me
once again

he continues
to make himself available
if he didn't remotely feel the same
he wouldn't be here

right?

- simulation

celia sinclair & e.m. handly

do I have the will or the means
to release my heart
from the confines of this prison
I meticulously built around it

peering through the steel bars
doesn't seem fair
typical case of mistaken identity

remembering the cries of lost souls
who helped cage me
in this cement cell

is there a chance to escape
this hell I have created
or am I damned to serve
a life sentence

- solitary confinement

love and other company

I see

I will

I did

I am

- love

her heart dangled
like raw meat
teasing the salivating
mouth of a wild dog
and tears of affirmation
fell from her lids

- awareness

love and other company

two worlds
unknown to anyone else
seem to have collided

we've always sensed
the other was there
dreamt
felt
seen
the other side

now somehow
we are thinking
feeling
melding
together

-jay

jason

she has returned

the brave one
picking up the rock
to find the snake
coiled underneath

the bold one
greeting the stray dog
eager to pet him

the innocent one
elated with encouragement
from those close to her heart

the curious one
wanting to feel everything
anything
that brings her joy

the little girl in me
can once again
dance, sing, and
play in the rain
recalling memories of freedom
never-ending security

someone has released her
someone has reminded her
that she is safe to give
all of the love
she has inside and
see – feel – know
she too is loved

- a child again

we watched the clouds
roll over us as they
engulfed the sky

each their own dance
all moving
to the same song

the rain slowly
assaulted our skin
giving fair warning
of what was to come

we listened to Mozart
while we drank
the wine of the witch
freely frolicking in tandem

the chemistry
between our souls
nearing the intensity
of the thunder

the harder the rain fell
the deeper the passion grew
both setting to accomplish
what it was destined to do

- the storm

celia sinclair & e.m. handly

we had it good at first
or so I thought
you didn't think so
you wouldn't have left

still you make a point
to come around
sometimes

could we be sexual soul mates
something's there otherwise
you wouldn't be here

what is it that brings you back
and why do I love you
as if you never left

- magnetic

love and other company

it's relieving to have found you
someone who thinks the way I think
feels the way I feel

I keep expecting to wake
at any moment
from this wonderful dream

still trying to decide
if being a hopeless romantic
is a blessing or a curse

at this moment the world is beautiful
the chirping of the birds
the sun shining above

surrounded by my screened in porch
my coffee tastes the best
it ever has

- morning joe

celia sinclair & e.m. handly

remember our lives
before us
the mad cash
our friends
the endless nights
of partying

we had such fun
then
no worries no cares
no arguments
or disagreements

we were so much in love
and wanted so much
to get away from it all
and just be
us

and we would sit up all night
over wine and lines
and talk about how
no one understood us
how real we were
and wished so much
for others to be

love and other company

now here we are without
much money to throw around
friends turned to acquaintances
late-night jam sessions traded in
for dirty diapers and spit-up

but I realize how real we are
still wish so much for others to be
and we would give anything
for us

- us

celia sinclair & e.m. handly

on the nights your away
the crickets keep me company

they sing to the moon
shining on the rave party
of fire flies in the field below

night after night
I watch the guest list
slowly diminish
the season of their dance
soon coming to an end

they have yet to invite me
still I watch and pretend
I am in their world

- other company

love and other company

I peer into my own eyes knowing,
I did everything I could.
I was always faithful.
I always put us first.
I tried my best to make you happy.
I did my best to prove
not all women are like her.

- reflection

celia sinclair & e.m. handly

---

*I just wanted you to love me
the way I loved you.*

I wish you could feel your actions
rip my heart through my throat

feel the pain in my tears
the worry on my brain
the weight of my soul
on the days you can be
so insensitive

I am sorry to have placed
such a burden on you
I'm sorry I forced you
into something
you're not ready for

or rather something
you never really wanted

- deception

celia sinclair & e.m. handly

I truly believed in our world
you really did make me feel
like a child again
and I would have given
anything
for us

I hope you find
whatever it is
you're looking for
I am so sorry
I could not give it to you

- crushed

oh the rage
the distrust
bestowed upon me

how to begin
the process
of recovery

you ripped my fucking heart out
spit on it before it hit the floor

made my dreams seem like
they were nothing more than
a mere fantasy

may you never forget the pain
you've inflicted upon me
and I – will forever be grateful

- broke

love and other company

wrath circles my heart
at this moment
this moment has lasted
for some time now

each time I see you
the knife twists
harder and deeper
into the core of my soul

black pools of hatred
churn in the pit of my stomach
twirling uncontrollably
searching desperately for a portal
to release itself and begin
the slow process
of recuperation

- enraged

may each tear
that falls from my lids
wash away another fear

make the heart stronger
the mind more clear

- mend

love and other company

manipulation, lies, betrayal
coercion, degradation

sincerity, longing, apathetic

drunkenness, brutality, distrust

passion, sensitivity, love
mischief, rage

forgiveness, tolerance
fear

hope, aspirations
self-pity

contempt, content, strife
adherence, loathing
happiness…

Reality.

- emotional upheaval

I've escaped the box
you maliciously tried to
enclose around me

still hear the criticisms
feel the disrespect you
so casually throw in my face
with a tainted look and
that coy grin of victory

a victory you will never claim

I'm taking back my power
my strength
my truth

what was your sword
will one day be nothing more
than a mere thorn in my side
easily plucked
like an annoying splinter
from a meaningless
piece of driftwood

- not a victim

love and other company

Do I offer too much,
or not enough?

Am I this insecure?

I think they all have issues.

Or maybe,
it really is just me?

With every stab to the heart,
every piercing shot to the ego,
may I rise above and remember
I am the master of my fate.

love and other company

these feelings have been hidden
for some time now
so afraid to peer through
the stone surface
of bitter anger

peacefulness, trust
a regeneration of – love

I've wanted for so long
for a man to look at me again
like there isn't a single thing about me
he couldn't love

do I have anything left
to try this once again

- mike

mike

traveling a road
never ventured
but still seems
so familiar

fields sway peacefully
granting wild flowers
to quietly reproduce

anxiously anticipating
the next turn like a child
kneeling in the back seat
of her parent's car

eyes wide
mouth gaping
inquisitively demanding
are we there yet

landmarking
what seems to be
the smoothest ride yet

without fear
the peddle hits the floor
splendidly speeding
ignoring all caution signs

celia sinclair & e.m. handly

dangerous curves ahead
watch for falling rock

a thoughtfully worthless attempt
to pace the rhapsody
of the wind

- loves journey

love and other company

been so long
since this heart has felt

are you even still beating
I swear I heard you today

don't come out yet
I'm not quite sure it's safe

has it been that long
since we've seen spontaneity
only time will tell
if we remember how

this loose-leaf has been burned
with a wax seal

how has anyone stumbled across
this dusty antique under lock and key
and why in the fuck would
anyone want to explore it

- relic

fits of insecurity and paranoia
continue to gnaw their way
to the surface

peeling away pieces of my brain
with vamp-like fangs
feeding on the flesh
that only so recently healed itself
from a previous attack

what shall become of me
should the evil thoughts reign
this blood bath of the mind

- time heals nothing

love and other company

I told you I'd be fine

for a while your manipulations
pummeled the person I used to be
clear into the center of a swirling
pool of disgust

wondering if I could ever escape
the relentless circles of madness
all the while trying to decide
if I wanted to

logic is far too close
a friend of mine

I fail to realize why you're here
heaven forbid it be as simple as
you want to be

there must be a hidden agenda
you must want something more
than me

- forgive me

love and other company

the words dangle from my tongue
afraid to slide down my chin
wiped away never to be spoken

should I reveal the feelings
that are choking me
like wine in my windpipe

and risk the humiliation
of a dumbfounded response

- hesitation

The portal has once again
been opened.

Are you ready to see
the other side?

the words have been spoken
yet the fear still lies

insecurities overwhelm me
and I think
I think too fucking much

I'm at my mind's mercy again
what was once so clear
has fallen into a fog of confusion

- overcomplicate

celia sinclair & e.m. handly

Clusters of memories
reign current thoughts.

Of which shall I allow
to win this grueling battle?

love and other company

wanting so badly
to be loved
it is here
isn't it

would god be so cruel
to blind-side me again

my heart
can't handle
another beating

- afraid

it's all coming back to me
the lies and manipulation
how quickly you turn it around

I know where I stand
I know what is right
this is not my fault

I refuse to do it alone
again

the weight isn't mine
to carry

- heavy

it was only a matter of time
before the sweet midday
phone calls would stop

only a matter of time
before I started to
cramp your style

it was only a matter of time
before you chose your friends
before me

although you pretended
to have wanted this
it was only a matter of time
before you realized
what you committed to

I knew it was only a matter of time
before you would give in to your fears
and walk away

- inevitable

I am not alone
yet I appear to be

my heart still suffers

wishing to light a candle
under the full moon
with my shadow next to me

receive all the answers
to my questions

- why

love and other company

you're here but it feels
as if you're already gone

it pains me to know
I was last on your list

at least your intensions hurt me
instead of your fist

celia sinclair & e.m. handly

the heart is so fragile
broken bones feel better
the pain is too familiar

a vice grip inside my chest
turning with every tear

I try to keep them in
making it more unbearable

how did this happen again
so close to my previous loss

I thought I was stronger
thought I had a plan
to repel this insanity

-regression

love and other company

so many pieces taken from me
others transformed

dreams shattered
beliefs found to be frauds

true love, soul mates
did *I* once speak these words

wish I remembered how it felt
to believe

can't trust myself
must pick up the remnants
bind them forever

- done

continue the journey in And Yet I Feel

*For more information visit
www.emhandly.com or
www.celiasinclair.net*

www.ingramcontent.com/pod-product-compliance
Lightning Source LLC
Chambersburg PA
CBHW020257030426
42336CB00010B/814